MESSAGE
FROM THE MOON

and other poems

MESSAGE
FROM THE MOON

and other poems

written and illustrated by

HILDA OFFEN

troika books

For Maisie Carter

Published by TROIKA BOOKS
First published 2017
1 3 5 7 9 10 8 6 4 2
Text and illustrations copyright © Hilda Offen 2017
The moral rights of the author/ illustrator have been asserted
All rights reserved
A CIP catalogue record for this book is available from the British Library
ISBN 978-1-909991-43-9
Printed in Poland

Troika Books
Well House, Green Lane, Ardleigh CO7 7PD, UK
www.troikabooks.com

Contents

From Dawn to Dusk

Outside in

Oh, Really?

Killer Caterpillar

There's a killer caterpillar on the loose!
He's hairy and he's striped with pink and puce.
He's longer than a bus –
At least twenty metres plus.
There's a killer caterpillar on the loose!

The killer caterpillar's dynamite!
He's tucking into everything in sight.
He's chewed off grandad's beard
And the hamster's disappeared.
The killer caterpillar's dynamite!

The killer caterpillar's seeing red!
He's eaten all the chairs and half my bed.
Now he's wriggling up the street
On his scary, hairy feet.
The killer caterpillar's seeing red!

The killer caterpillar's on the prowl!
You'll know him by his rumbly, grumbly growl.
So don't go into town –
He's sure to hunt you down.
The killer caterpillar's on the prowl!

The Animal Talent Show

First on stage is the Carolling Cow.
You must see her perform – she's a wow!
Her trilling's so thrilling
They gave her top billing.
Bravo! Singing cow – take a bow!

Next up is the Juggling Goat.
She's wearing a pink petticoat.
Six mangos, a pear –
She keeps them all in the air,
As well as a frog and a stoat.

Here's Harry the Fox-trotting Horse!
His fan-club are all out in force.
See him dance the fandango,
The waltz and the tango –
(His partner's a pony, of course).

Last of all is the Musical Sheep.
She arrived at the show in a jeep.
She's playing the flute,
Kettle-drums and a lute.
(Signed photos are all going cheap).

Alien 1

As I was walking my dog Shah,
I met a stranger from a distant star.
His face was green, his eyes were red –
Two curly horns grew from his head.
His hand was like a tuning fork –
He raised it and prepared to talk.
He struck a pose and gave a speech,
Delivered in a piercing screech.
He said "Gloop-gluggo! Gloopy-gloo!
Oogly-poogly, woogly-woo!
Floogle-woogle, woffly-floff!"
But then Shah barked and he ran off.

I travelled far, through time and space.
I met a stranger in an alien place.
His eyes shone with a mystic light;
He looked alert – and keen – and bright.
He trailed a creature on a lead –
It shook and trembled like a reed.
I gave a stirring speech of greeting
To honour this historic meeting.
The alien spoke. Through ruffled fur,
He said "Bow-wow! Woof-woof!" and "Grrr!"
But when he lunged and snarled "Yip-yip!"
I legged it for the mother ship.

The Troll Speaks Out

That's not how it happened!
Now I've had enough –
I'm dishing the dirt
On the Billy Goats Gruff.

There was no 'Fol-de-Rol',
No field of green grass,
No rickety bridge –
The whole thing's a farce.

I was tending my roses,
(I'd mended the bridge),
When I saw the three goats
Coming over the ridge.

I went forward to meet them,
My arms open wide.

"I've got some Swiss roll –
Won't you all come inside?"

14

One suddenly charged;
It was like a bad dream.
I flew through the air,
Landing 'Splosh!' in the stream.

By the time I crawled out,
All covered in gunk,
They'd eaten my roses
And then done a bunk.

And that's the plain truth –
It's the worst of all scandals!
Those Billy Goats Gruff
Are nothing but vandals.

The Dragon

Who am I? What am I?
I've no way of knowing,
Folded here in the dark.
But my shoulder-blades itch
And I know that I'm growing,
Folded here in the dark.

CRACK

Where am I? I blink –
The light hurts my eyes.
None the wiser, unsure,
I unfurl in the sun.

But look! I have talons
Of bright, burnished brass –
Green scales that glitter
Like glass in the light.
Flame flows through my veins;
I stretch – I breathe fire!
My wings tremble above me;
I spread them – I soar!

Now the world streams beneath me.
I roar - and I **ROAR!**

Three Little Monsters

Here's a little monster –
His face is blue.
He's jumping up and down,
Shouting "What shall we do?"

Here's a little monster -
His face is pink.
He's found some lemonade
And he's having a drink.

Here's a little monster –
His face is red.
He wears a party hat
And he's standing on his head.

Three little monsters,
Red and pink and blue.
They hide in a cupboard
Then they all shout BOO!

The Robber Rabbit

I am a robber rabbit!
If I see your bag I'll grab it.
I'm a burglar, I'm a bounder –
A criminal all-rounder.

I'm a conman, I'm a conjuror,
A pilferer, a plunderer –
I'm a raider, I'm a rustler,
A hoodlum and a hustler.

I'm a deadly desperado,
Brimming over with bravado!
I'm a cracksman! I'm a crook!
Before you've time to look

I'll sneak up and pick your pocket
And shoot off like a rocket.
Hah! By the time the police come round
I'll be safely underground.

"You're a bad boy, Jack!
Now – take it all back!"

Feathers and Fur

Tiger, Tiger!

Tiger, Tiger! Go away!
You've followed me around all day –
Into school and out to play.
Tiger, Tiger! Go away!

Tiger, Tiger! It's not fair!
Every time I look, you're there –
In my bath or in my chair.
Tiger, Tiger! It's not fair.

Wild Geese

We heard their conversation first;
Then, over the low hill to our right,
The geese came rowing into view.
On they came, holding the crescent moon
In the wide V of their flight.
We watched them pass above us,
Then navigate the valley's scoop,
The rock-face and the quarry walls,
Until the echoes faded into mist
And everything was quiet.

The grass moved at our feet
Like the waves of the sea.
And above us, the moon
Stood alone in the sky.

Fox

Flame flicker,
Russet flash
Upon bracken banks,
You watch the trains –
Calm as a Buddha,
Smiling, narrow-eyed.

Deep-chested,
Rabbit-fed, replete,
With forepaws neatly placed –
Your presence strikes us dumb.
You are a revelation,
You flickering tongue of fire.

We are your shadow-world:
Your commonplace.

Crow

Dark pantalooned dandy,
He struts the lawn
On elevated heels.
Sleek as an oil-slick,
Fastidious, precise,
Pointing his slender toes.
At his approach
The small birds scatter
As though a king
Has come amongst them.

It's an illusion.
Suddenly he's changed –
A king no longer,
But a bully-boy.
He chases interlopers,
Pecking, threatening,
Shatters the morning
With his raucous cry.

Raven

Once you were Wotan's bird.
Harsh-voiced, trident-headed,
You ranged the battlefields,
Gorging your fill.
Night-black, pitch-black,
Black as yourself you are.
Yes – once you were Wotan's bird –
Look at you now!

Clip-winged, lop-sided,
Walled in the Tower.
Once heroes were your feast;
Now any crumb will do.
Your liege is lost, long-lost –
The Ravenmaster pens you up at night.
That croak, your former battle-cry,
Makes children laugh and point.
Look at you now!

The Reading Dogs

Friday afternoons are cool!
The Reading Dogs come into school.
They wag their tails, their soft eyes glisten –
We read to them and they just listen.
They don't butt in, 'tut-tut' or sigh
And snap 'That's wrong! Try harder! Try!'

Joe is a golden labrador.
He sits beside me on the floor:
And if I stumble on a word,
He smiles as though he hasn't heard.
My teacher's pleased. Last week she said

My goodness, Josh! You're miles ahead!
You started off with Bob the Builder
And now you're halfway through Matilda!

BUT –

Here's what my teacher doesn't know -
We have a secret, me and Joe.
For what Miss Parker doesn't see
Is Joe, my dog, reading to **me**.

He growls on at an awesome rate –
He doesn't trip or hesitate.
If there's a word he doesn't know,
He'll just say 'Ruff!' and on he'll go.
The Witches, Stig, The Gruffalo –
We've read them all, have me and Joe.
I sit and dream and stroke his fur
And listen to his gentle burr.

But when he thinks I've had enough
Joe wags his tail and says

Herons

That's where they landed:
The servants shipped the oars
And there was laughter
And the swish of silk,
The flash of jewelled brocade.
And music! Something silvery and soft –
The threads of violins and flutes
Went weaving through the reeds;
Then fading, faded, sinking in the silt.

But now the inheritors –
The heirs of the wetlands,
The water and the wild air –
The sombre-suited herons
Dream their story,
Among the bleached, wind-rippled reeds.
Or in those trees,
Clotted with dark nests,
They brood, world-weary and aloof,
Indifferent to the clacking crowds below.

One emissary breasts the blast
And rides the air
With condescending, loping strokes.
Over the sluice-gates,
Wind-buffeted, he braves the gusts
And fades into the trees.

Dream-Time

After the Fireworks

We came home late,
After the fireworks.
I was so tired,
My head was spinning.

Down, down I dropped,
Into the dormer window –
And (much to my surprise)
My pod, glass-fronted
And softly cushioned,
Wrenched itself away
From the creaking house –
And off we lurched
Across the Weald,
While all the while white fires
Cartwheeled across the sky.
Rockets exploded in my brain
And something called
"Come on! Come on!"
So on we reeled on stilted legs,
Onwards and onwards,
Under the reign of stars.

Message from the Moon

We parted from you in the mists of time.
You are our mother, the great blue planet,
Poised on our horizon like a lamp –
Ever-constant, ever-changing,
There in the blackness of the sky.
We watch you turn upon your axis,
While white clouds streak your oceans
And spread from pole to pole.
We watch you through your phases;
Waxing full, your earth-shine lights us;
Your darkening is never an eclipse,
Only a gauzy veil, with silver sparks
Speckling your continents.

Once, long ago, you sent us visitors.
We saw them stumble from their craft,
Take giant steps across our barren rocks,
Leap, turn and land and leap again.
We stayed well out of sight,
Shadowed by the crater's rim;
Waiting, waiting, till they'd done.
And then we watched them leave.

Above us the stars still rise and set,
Tracing their arcs across the silent sky.

The Brekpop Pack

"Tim!" says Mum. "It's time for school!
Stop dreaming! Eat your cereal!"
My Brekpops crackle in the milk,
But something else has caught my eye.
I'm studying the Brekpop pack;
For on that pack there is a boy –
A boy who looks a bit like me.
(His hair's too bright,
His skin's too pink;
My teeth will never be that white)
But otherwise, he looks like me,
I think.

He's holding up a Brekpop pack!
And on that pack there is a boy,
A boy with custard-coloured hair,
Who's holding up a Brekpop pack -
(A boy who looks a bit like me.)
And on his pack there is a boy.
A smaller boy with rosy cheeks;
He's holding up another pack
(That boy who looks a bit like me) .
And on his pack a smaller boy,
A boy with teeth
Of dazzling white,
Is holding up
A Brekpop pack
And on
His
Pack ...

TIM! COME ON!

shouts Mum.

The Apple Tree

The great gale
Brought me down.
Once I was a citadel –
Anchored in earth,
I rode the years,
Weathered the rainstorms
And the winter winds.
Birds thronged my boughs,
Cats stalked my mossy paths;
The fox stole by in starlight,
Sparkling in the frost.

Do you remember me?
I am still here –
Here in the garden,
Silvered by the moon.
Do you hear echoes?
Echoes of birdsong,
Of blossom,
Soft rustles, laughter,
The heavy thud of fruit?

I am still here.

What She Remembers

What she remembers are the great horses
And him leading them into the yard;
How he hoisted her onto the broad-backed Sol
And how she once rode the world like a queen.

She remembers her mother – "Coo-up! Coo-up!"
As she called in the Indian Runners;
And how the stately, long-necked ducks
Came filing back home through the corn.

And now she remembers the tithe barn
Where he looped cart-ropes over the beams
And how she swung in the hay-scented air
While dust-motes glittered in the shafts of sun.

She thinks she remembers the well, where once
They lowered him down to rescue a dog.
It was so dark, that when he looked up
He said he could see the stars.

Then he went away to the War.
And afterwards everything changed.

Staying Awake

I'm going to stay awake all night!
I'll watch the foxes
Sneaking round the bins
And see the neighbours' cats
Prowling on midnight walls.

I'm going to stay awake all night!
I want to lie and listen
To the hush in the house
And hear the church clock
Striking every hour.

I'm going to .. zz .. zz ..

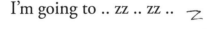

Dawn to Dusk

Day-break

Darkness flies from the river;
It thickens and curdles,
Clogging the broad eaves.
The bats are cominq home to roost.

There are shades in the shallows –
White wraiths, willow-shrouded.
Rinsed with light, egrets rise
And wing over water.

The Sea

I breathe in –
A deep, slow AAAH!
I draw the tide
To meet the sky.

I leave mementos in my wake –
Sand-ripples, shining pools,
Ghost crabs and feathers,
Drifts of shell and shingle;
Seaweed spread like tresses,
Mermaids' purses, bladder-wrack
And drops of emerald glass.

I hold my breath.

Now castles rise;
Cloud shadows race
Across the sands.
Fish flap in rock-pools,
Kites soar, gulls scream
And children laugh.
Well – let them laugh;
I've time.

At last I sigh -
PHEEEW!

The tide flows back
And castles crumble –
Moats fill with foam
And towers collapse.
Seaweed, feathers, float
Upon my lapping waves.
I'm back! I'm back
To greet the shore.

Freezing Fog

Beechwoods blossom.
Ghost ships loom
Through the white air.
Schooners in full sail
Billow above us –
Bloom forward
On their frost journey.

The Stranger

Winter's sliding away.
Trees are still threadbare,
Patched with black nests –
But faint blossom
Threads through the hedges
And here and there
A thorn mistakes its cue
And bursts into green fire.

Dogwood smoulders
And willows redden;
Now the sun comes slanting
Across the cold fields
And the spring sidles in
Like a stranger,
Through the half-open door
Of the year.

The Peppermint Path

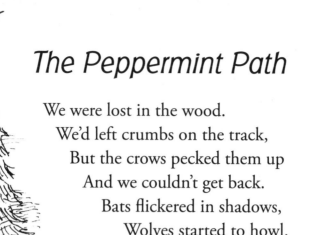

We were lost in the wood.
　We'd left crumbs on the track,
　　But the crows pecked them up
　　And we couldn't get back.
　　　Bats flickered in shadows,
　　　　Wolves started to howl.
　　　　There were mutterings, scutterings –
　　　Things on the prowl.
　　We were tired, we were hungry,
　　Ice-cold and alone.
　Red eyes pierced the dark;
Winds started to moan.

All at once the trees parted
　And that's when we saw
　　A gingerbread house
　　　With a wide-open door.
　　　　Its roof tiles were dusted
　　　　　With sugar and spice,
　　　　　The window-sills carved
　　　　Out of coconut ice.
　　　Chimneys of caramel!
　　Butterscotch beams!
　We stared, open-mouthed,
At a house made of dreams.

So we started to follow
  The peppermint path;
    Past the marzipan door
      Blazed a welcoming hearth.
    The heat warmed our cheeks –
    It was drying our tears –
   And that's when a voice called
"Come in, little dears!"

Night-time

Skateboard sears the night –
Soars over speed-humps,
Each one a comma
In its clattering flight.
There on the viaduct
Trains meet and merge,
Then draw apart,
Like chains of golden beads.

The sable hollow of the town
Is pierced with lights –
With dazzling galaxies
And neon constellations –
Moving, glowing, still.

The night is full of stars,
Of stories. Somewhere
A siren wails.

Outside-In

Bad Hair Day

I sit here on a kitchen chair
While Doris Driscoll cuts my hair.
She talks and talks; she doesn't stop
And all the while it's chop! chop! chop!
I offer up a silent prayer -
"Please, Doris Driscoll – spare my hair!"
She tells my Mum the latest news –
Who's fallen ill, who's got new shoes.
Her silver scissors flash and clip
And whirl and twirl and snip! snip! snip!
The pile of hair below my chair
Grows deeper – deeper. It's not fair.
But round and round the chair she stalks
And clips and combs and talks and talks.

What I would like is nice long hair
That floats behind me in the air.
Hair I could curl, hair I could plait.
(Fat chance of that, with all this chat).
She waves a mirror and I cringe.
My hair's a joke – and where's my fringe?

Oh! Let me melt into thin air
When Doris comes to cut my hair.

Sally Small

My name is Sally Small
And I like to walk on walls.

They all say "Silly Sally!
Come along – don't dilly-dally!"
But my name is Sally Small
And I like to walk on walls.

Mum says "Sally Small! Get down!
We've got to get to town!"
But my name is Sally Small
And I walk best on a wall.

My Gran says "Silly Sally!
Jump on down – don't shilly-shally!"
But my name is Sally Small
And I have to walk this wall.

They say "Please hurry, Sally!
We've got to get to ballet!"
I'm afraid they'll have to wait –
I need to concentrate.

I'm practising to walk a rope
Across Niagara Falls!
My name is Sally Small
And I like to walk on walls.

Betrayed

My sister said "I love you, Chubby-Chops."
She squeezed my cheek, she looked me in the eye.
"I love you deep as oceans, high as hills –
And if a mad giraffe was on the prowl
I'd rescue you. And if a hungry lion
Was after you, he could have me instead.
And if an elephant was sitting down on you,
I'd push you clear – and he could sit on me."

Last week, my friend Bill Jones and I
Were trapped up on the bank
By Nobby Tiler's gang.
They kept on throwing mud at us.
We couldn't get away.
Bill Jones was crying. (So was I).
Just then, I saw my sister in the road.
She looked at me – straight in the eye.

And then she ran away.

So now I know.
Giraffes and giants and polar bears,
Dragons and vampires, elephants and lions:
If they're about, I just don't stand a chance –
Not if my sister's there. "Here, lion!" she'd say.
"Have Chubby-Chops, he's tastier than me.
Tired, Mr Elephant? Sit here – he's nice and soft."

And then she'd run away.

The Visit

After school last Friday,
Someone rang our bell.
And there upon the doorstep
Stood Kevin, Dan and Del.

(I wish I'd never said it –
Why did 1 tell them that?
But Del and Kev have rabbits
And Daniel's got a rat).

"Where is he?" shouted Kevin.
"Where is he?" shouted Dan.
They ran into the living-room
And then the search began.

They looked inside the cupboards;
They rummaged everywhere.
They looked behind the curtains,
They looked beneath each chair.

"Well! We give up!" growled Kevin.
"Come on – where is he, then?"
And all three yelled together :
"SO – WHERE'S YOUR OSTRICH, BEN?"

That's when I had a bright idea;
I cried out in dismay:
"Oh no! The window's open!
He must have flown away!"

The Trail

A snail's in the house!
Look – a silvery trail!
Dad gave a bellow
And Mum gave a wail.

"Did he sneak through the cat-flap –
Stow away with the greens?"
"He's crawled through the wardrobe
And ruined my jeans!"

"I'll put some beer in a saucer,"
Dad said with a frown.
"That'll fix him, the blighter!
He'll fall in and drown."

We were woken next day
By a furious roar.
Dad had spotted a trail
Snaking all round the floor.

It climbed to the ceiling,
Right over the bed.
Dad was crimson with rage.
"I don't believe it!" he said.

The trail curled and twisted
Like silvery ink.
Then the curls turned to words:

Morning!. Thanks for the drink......

Don't!

Do **not** pour custard on your toast –
It's gloopy and it's runny.
Just save it for your apple pie –
You're better off with honey.

Do **not** rub honey in your hair –
It's gooey and it's icky.
Moreover, it attracts the flies –
Shampoo is much less sticky.

Do **not** pour shampoo in your shoes –
It's slippery and it's wet.
You'd squish and squelch about the house –
Socks are a better bet.

Don't drop your socks into the flan,
Or add a pot of mustard.
They will do nothing for the taste –
Why don't you try some custard?

But –

Last Word

At my approach, the forests shake,
The grasslands quiver, mountains quake.
Well might you stare – when did you see
Such bulk, such power, such majesty?
And what are you? A speck, a dot.

But you're extinct. And I am not.

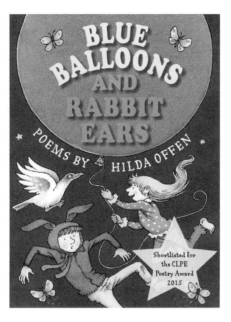

Blue Balloons and Rabbit Ears

This is award-winning illustrator Hilda Offen's
first collection of her own poems and has been
shortlisted for the CLiPPA Poetry Award.

*'The playful title perfectly captures the spirit of this delightful collection.
Readily accessible through their strong adherence to rhythm and rhyme,
the poems' subject matter will appeal to a wide age range … a collection
which children can return to for many years.'* – **Carousel**

*'An appealing collection for young children, illustrated by the poet.
Full of fun and rhyme and rhythm and a variety of verse forms, it includes
thoughtful themes about nature and history too.'* – **CLiPPA judges**

*'An enticing mix of original nursery rhymes and poems
to entertain all ages.'* – **Parents in Touch**